Made in United States
North Haven, CT
04 September 2023

41135030R00078